DEDICATION

To Mia, your world is mine and mine is yours. Together, we will travel the world, once city at a time. I love you.

Table of Contents

CHAPTER 1- ACCEPTING EMOTIONS AS PART OF HUMAN NATURE

Emotions are already a part of human nature. But how much do you really know about emotions? What are emotions? What are their elements? What are the most common types of emotions? This chapter is where you will learn the basics of emotions for you to get started.

Emotions seem to be like a king that rules your day to day life. The decisions that you make are based on whether you are happy, sad, bored, frustrated or angry. Your hobbies and activities are chosen based on the kind of emotions that they incite. But what exactly are emotions?

By definition, emotions are complex psychological states involving three unique components: subjective experience, physiological response and expressive or behavioral response.

Aside from trying to understand what exactly emotions are, the researchers also tried identifying and classifying the various types of emotions. Paul Eckman, a psychologist, suggested in 1972 that there are actually 6 basic emotions that can be considered universal in the entire human cultures, namely anger, fear, disgust, surprise, sadness, and happiness. But in 1999, he further expanded the list, including some other basic emotions such as excitement, embarrassment, contempt, pride, shame, amusement and satisfaction.

In the 1980s, Robert Plutchik introduced the so-called wheel emotions, another kind of emotion classification system. In this model, it was demonstrated how various emotions can be mixed or combined together, in the same way that artists combine the primary colors in order to come up with secondary colors. He suggested that there are actually eight primary emotional dimensions, including fear versus anger, sadness versus happiness, disgust versus trust and anticipation versus surprise. These emotions can then be mixed in various ways. For instance, anticipation and happiness can be combined to create excitement.

But what are really the purposes of your emotions? What do they do for you? Certainly, these have an important effect on you but what are these all for?

Motivation from Emotions

Your emotions motivate you. Without them, you will never be able to do much, thus, you will not survive, which is applicable to the evolved form that you are now. Your body can feel motivations. Your muscles either relax or tense. Your blood vessels contract or dilate. When you feel emotional, you can also feel this physically. It means that your emotions can either make you comfortable or uncomfortable, sending signals for you to do something right away or just stay in your comfortable state.

Emotions Act as Social Signals

In general, people wear their hearts on their sleeves as their inner emotions are being displayed on their outer bodies. Your face in particular has about 90 muscles wherein 30 have the main purpose of signaling your emotions to others. These signals are very useful for they let other people decide how to behave toward you. When you look angry, those around you will never think of attacking you.

Emotions as Internal Signals

For instance, internally, when you try to make a decision or understand something, you use your emotions to determine if your conclusion is a good idea. When you think of something that contradicts your values, your emotions are going to tell you that this is bad. When you think of something that can hurt you, your emotions are going to tell you that the idea is not good. By simply imagining what can happen, your emotions will be triggered, thus letting you come up with better decisions.

How to Evaluate Your Emotions without Professional Help

You feel messed up and instead of doing something to figure out the reason behind this, you just resort to telling yourself that life is really unfair and you are a terrible person. However, not being able to distinguish between your negative emotions and letting them lump together to form into a miserable mess can actually lead to great deals of emotional stress based on the latest study.

Experts say that those who find it difficult to distinguish one emotion from another usually have a sense of unpleasantness in general. If you cannot differentiate your emotions, you will find it harder to act in the appropriate way.

Keeping Emotions in Check

For you to get to the bottom of what you are truly feeling there are several things that you can try to straighten up your emotions.

Give yourself some time out. Every day, try to allot some time for decompression. Take note that you have no capacity of reacting properly to a certain situation when you still carry the emotions of the earlier time in your day.

You can try training your emotional brain. Not all people have the ability of identifying their emotions that are more nuanced but you can at least try honing your skills by starting with what you can. Try identifying your emotions beyond what is unpleasant. Is it guilt? Anger? Or shame? Simply asking these questions can already help you in pinpointing your angst.

Write things down. When you find it hard to identify your various emotions, try to jot down your feelings. Patterns will start to form that can help you in differentiating one emotion to another.

Check your gut. Are you reacting to a physical sensation or to an emotion? When doubtful, rule out the physical causes of your feelings such as hunger and lack of sleep.

Take a stroll. You probably think that your busy day is over once you walk out the door but if you still have a racing pulse; chances are your emotional state is still controlled by your physiology. Taking a walk is the best choice when it comes to emotional regulation. This directs your attention inward, helping you to refocus.

Clean up your clutter. Having a clean and tidy space will be able to help you focusing your thoughts where they are required to be. Mental or physical clutter can both add to your overall sense of disarray. If you find it hard to focus, the mere act of cleaning and its result will be able to help in clearing your mind.

Chapter 2- Commanding Your Emotions by Understanding Where They Come From

The emotions are not an easy task to master. To command the emotions you need some intense abilities to look inside you and pull up some of your leadership qualities to put the mind to work. Emotions are feeling packed thoughts that stem from the heart. The heart is deceiving and will mislead the mind, thus to understand emotions you have to go deep and beyond and put your emotions to the test by understanding and controlling the heart. Still, emotions are good-working sources provided to us through a wonderful creation. It is possible to understand the emotions, which could lead you to command the emotions and become the master of your mind. Yet, what does it take?

It takes removing doubts, lies, deceit, hate, envy, and all those ugly other words out of your head and heart. If you have traps, blind spots, or tripping triggers you will not master, nor command the emotions to do anything. Now, we can go on many levels to command and master the emotions, however we can start with the basics for now.

Because the mind wanders and thinks, the emotions feed from the heart and mind. IF the head has lies, it will affect the heart and emotions, which in turn puts the emotions in control and you on the backlines trying to figure it out. Still, you have an inner child within that either helps you or else harms you.

Today we are going to work on your inner child. The inner child is the person that you left standing in childhood and that still plays a vital part in your mind, emotions and heart. If you have impulsive response, thus it is because you have an inner child driving you feelings and/or emotions. Most times these impulses will infringe on other people's rights and may even hurt their feelings. This is at what time you unleash the leader inside you to gain control. The problem is you have practiced obeying those impulses.

The key is to practice to control your impulses by controlling your child within. The more you practice the more your emotions and heart, as well as your feelings stemmed from the heart and emotions will obey your commands. A person that has not mastered his emotions will often make other people's life miserable. Most times these people live for the minute, instead of taking it one day at a time. The person often views his/her loved ones as slaves while he/she dictates their every move. Sometimes the behaviors lead to excessive alcohol usage, drug usage, excessive eating, poor diet, tempers, uncontrolled emotions, and a saddened heart. How can you overcome this behavior? You can turn those impulses and slaving emotions into a positive force.

Now you are the slave of your emotions. You must take control of these emotions. This means you will need to develop that child within you and retrain the child so that he/she begins to see that maturity has to take place. It's time to grow up child.

Impulses are not a bad mechanism. In fact, we have impulses incorporated into our personality. In truth, it is a natural element. Impulses are inspiring mechanisms, motivating sources, and a force that communicates to our minds in an effort to promote actions. For instance, your friend asks you to go to the movies and your favorite film is showing, you impulsively say yes and rush out the door to go to the theatre. You acted on impulse in this instance without forethought likely. Now, if you would have seated self, thought about the request, consequences and your surrounding responsibilities before responding, you would have commanded your emotions, mastered your thoughts and unleashed the leader inside you. The first scene shows your child coming to the fore, while the second scene shows maturity taking control. Unleashing the mind is a step in commanding and mastering the emotions.

Where Do Emotions Come From?

Do you know where your emotions are coming from? In the same way that you cannot understand why a certain person acts like that when you do not know his or her background, you will also not be able to comprehend your emotions when you do not know where they come from in the first place. By understanding where your emotions are coming, emotional balance can become more possible.

There are some people who assume that your emotions are stemming from your thoughts. But the truth is; this is completely wrong as there is a little bit more involved than your thoughts alone. Your emotions are not only about what you think about or how you put your attention to them. In contrast to some of the present self-help philosophy, a person's emotions do not only come from his or her thoughts alone.

Did you ever experience listening to a comedian who tells his tragic story while adding a sense of fun to it? Comedians have this skill of discussing their relationship breakups, the collapse of the economy or even war in such a way that makes you laugh about it. These people make you think of tragedies and laugh with true joyful emotions regarding them. Obviously, there is something more than the subject matter or thoughts to create emotions. In a way, something in your point of view can affect the emotions that you create.

On the other hand, in some other moments that you think about a breakup, an economic challenge or war, it is no longer funny. You quickly feel anger, sadness, despair and injustice. If you believe that it is only your thoughts or what you put your attention on is what creates emotions, then you have accepted a plain answer and give up on the real truth.

Among the truths that people overlook is that you are the one that creates your emotions. This is overlooked because there are instances when they say things like "That is frightening" or "She is the reason for my happiness." These things sound as if other people or situations created your emotions, without a mention of yourself being the one responsible for a certain aspect of this process. Believing such thoughts or comments can make you overlook your role in creating your emotions.

Another thing that can affect your emotions is your point of view that you use when observing a thought. Comedians have the humorous perspective regarding tragic events that can make you laugh when you look at it from their viewpoint. Politicians discuss a similar situation using a viewpoint invoking a feeling or righteousness or patriotism. Meanwhile, the point of view of the victim looking at the similar situation will cause him or her to feel sad. The point of view you use for perceiving events or from where your thoughts come from can affect the emotions that you create.

It is not only what you are thinking about but more about the viewpoint you think about this from that leaves an impact. Depending on the viewpoint that you have, you can come up with different interpretations thus making you believe various assumptions. Beliefs are then formed when you believed in these assumptions and interpretations or these activate your existing beliefs which can also have an effect on the emotions that you make as well as the level of their strength.

Your emotions are a powerful energy form or power and this comes from faith, a kind of personal power that can turn your thought to a belief. Thoughts have no power but beliefs have the power of the faith that you have.

Thoughts are not enough for creating emotions. There are some thoughts that pass through your mind and there are instances when you find these thoughts funny. Later on, when you try to look at things from a different viewpoint, you feel different regarding an exactly same thing. Your most embarrassing moment when you were in high school might have been the worst nightmare of your life that week. But with a bigger perspective of time, say, 30 years after, it will just become nothing but a mere source of genuine laughter. Even after 30 years, the history of that event is still the same but over time, your perspective has already changed and together with this, your emotions also change.

The quality of your emotion in terms of pain or pleasure that you make will largely depend on how you look at things or your point of view. The emotions' intensity that you create during that moment will depend on the amount of faith that you invested in the assumptions and beliefs that support that thought. Faith in some beliefs is the power source behind every emotion that you have. Get your faith from all the beliefs that surround a thought and you will surely be able to alter the emotions that you feel.

The emotions that stem from your thoughts are the product of your point of view, your underlying beliefs and the amount of power that you put in them in the form of faith. In case you are trying to alter your emotional state through altering just your thoughts, you will never be able to succeed. Attempting to alter your emotions without changing your viewpoint, faith investment and underlying assumptions will probably fail. It will be like building a chair with a single leg and expecting this to give you the support that you need.

If you want to change your emotional reactions, emotional state and put more happiness into your life, it is a must that you change your point of view and recover your faith from the false beliefs that you have.

The Extent of Which It Is Acceptable to Carry Out Emotions

I would like to take the time to tell you how you can learn to command and master your emotions. No, you do not have to go to a therapist or nothing like that; you just have to learn that emotions are, only meant, to be carried out to a certain extent.

Let's begin with talking about sadness. I know that occasionally you have something in your life that causes you to feel sad, down and out. I have learnt that when something happens in your life you should just go with the flow. Even though you may be sad, you still have to live your life and move on. I know that, at the particular moment you feel like you could cry a river, and you should, but once you get it all out of your system, you should be able to look at the situation from another point of view.

The outside view, where you take the time to look at the situation from a wider angle, sometimes you are not able to prevent things from happening, sometimes situations are destined to occur and you can't do anything about it. That is part of life that you should just face and grow on. However, if there is something that you can do to prevent from being sad you should think about the things that make you sad and try to avoid them altogether, if you avoid the things that make you sad then you will not have to go through the hassle of dealing with those painful emotions.

The next emotion that I would like to talk to you about is happiness or joy. Happiness is at what time you can't stop smiling for anything in the world. It's as if someone painted a smile on your face and you just can't take it off. If you experience happiness, then you are one of the lucky ones, because most people don't even smile or laugh. I guess they don't have anything to smile or laugh about. Otherwise, something is seriously wrong in the mind. If you share the happiness you have with others make sure that you do not express your happiness too much. If you do then your friends may think that you are a little crazy. However, if you do not have any happiness, then you should work on finding things that make you feel a sense of happiness and start building on them so that you too can be happy with all the rest of us.

There is one emotion that I know is in every household, and that is anger. When things don't go your way, do you start blaming everyone else for your bad day? At this point, you shouldn't, if something makes you mad, cuss it out or beat it up, and don't blame the other people in your household because they are not the ones that made you mad. If one of your family members is to blame then you should avoid punishing them and go for a walk or a drive just to get away from things. Most times when a person is mad it is because they fail to have control of their minds. Anyone striking out at another person is only showing that he/she is not the master of his/her emotions and something within is in command.

Do You Know How to Master and Command Your Emotions?

Sometimes as human beings it is hard to command and master your emotions, that is why I hope that the information that I am about to share with you helps you out with your emotions and the struggle to command and master the mind. The emotions stem from feelings, which stem from the heart. At what time a person feels hurt they will often lash out, rather than gain control. Therefore, it takes you to control the mind and gain power of self.

In order to command your emotions, you must be able to understand what it is that you want to be, whether it is happy, mad, or sad. You are the only one that can control and command your emotions. If you want to be happy, then tell yourself that you are going to be happy today, if you want to be mad, then be mad and make everyone else mad too, if you want to be sad, express your feelings and understand that things can't get any worse, they can only get better.

In order to master your emotions you must be able to know what extent you can be stretch out to and then try not to be pushed to that point. If you are able to say, "I need to cool off" then you are on the road to success. If you are able to tell yourself that you know that something bad is going to happen if you don't cool off then you already know you're high and low points. All you have to do now is build on them.

Keeping Emotions in Check
I am going to tell you a couple of ways that you can help command and master your emotions.

1) Instead of getting mad and taking your emotions out on someone else, you should avoid the situation for a while. Do something that will take your mind off the situation until you can think clearer.

2) Instead of being sad and crying all the time, try to think about why the situation happened that made you feel sad, once you realize that it couldn't have been prevented then you will be able to understand and accept the situation. If the situation was a death that made you sad, then you have to keep the memories of the one you lost alive and remember all the good times you shared with that person and know that they love you.

3) Instead of being jealous, realize that if something does happen between you and the one that you love, that there are plenty of single people out there. Most importantly one of those people is meant for you. Just because the first relationship didn't work out doesn't mean that the next one won't. All men are different and all women are different. If you want to remain with that person you should try to work on things, talk to the other person about them so that you will be able to discuss how each other feels. I have learnt that in a relationship, you can't be with someone that you can't trust. If you are with someone that you can't trust then you are better to call it quits because you will always find yourself questioning his or her every move.

There are many ways to deal with emotions. It takes you to get in connection with your own mind so that you have some control. The mind can play tricks on you, accordingly getting in touch with your mind will help you spot those tricks. Being a parent requires how to command and master your emotions also.

Chapter 3- Controlling Your Emotions for Your Children

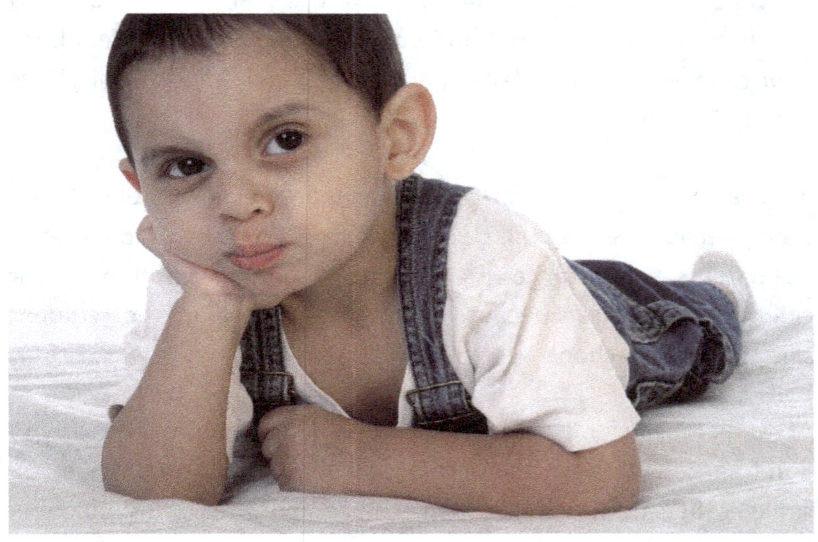

Being a parent is already hard enough without having to involve your emotions. Once your emotions kick in, you are in for a ride. As a parent, you will feel every emotion that is humanly possible because your children will take you there over the years and as these children grow, you will continue down the emotional path of raising children. It never ends!

At what time your children cry, you will cry because they are hurting physically and/or mentally. The only thing you can do however is to help them cope. Your children may cry because their puppy died, or their hamster ran away. These things may be little to you, but they mean the world to your children.

At what time your children are mad, you will be mad because someone has caused them to become angry. The only thing you can do is find out why they are mad and talk about why it made the child mad. Your children may be mad because they can't go to the park or because he or she lost their basketball game. Children often get mad for reasons, thus it is important to find out why.

At what time your child is in pain, you will feel pain because you are there mother or father and you don't want them to feel hurt. Your children may have fallen and scraped their knee or fell off his or her bike.

At what time your children are sad, you are going to feel sad with them, because, seeing the child hurt makes you hurt inside as well. As parents, importance is placed on sharing emotions. Your children may be sad because of something that another student said to them at school.

At what time your child is happy, you will be happy, even if you don't agree with what they are happy about, it still will make you smile. If they are happy about an achievement then you should feel happy with them and give them some kind of reward. This promotes good working emotions.

At what time your child does something wrong, then you should correct them because it is up to you to raise your children the way that you would want them to be raised. It is important to give positive discipline, rather than hurt, harm, or beat the child. A spanking is good, only at what time you have control of your own emotions. Beating a person will only lead to super major problems:

Being a parent is tough; however, there are ways that you can work harder to be a better parent. As a parent, you are entitled to feel emotions and express your feelings; you just want to make sure that you know the difference between the two.

If you work hard to learn how to command and master your emotions I am sure that you will be a better person overall. You don't have to be the sweetest mom, but you need to know that there is a place and time for everything.

I hope that you have found my information to be helpful and I hope that you will be able to learn from what I have said. I am sure there are going to be times that you wish you could just run away but you can't. If you know how to command and master your emotions then you should be able to be a wonderful parent and a wonderful wife and/or husband. Emotions are very tricky and sometimes you may not understand why you feel a certain way until something happens to confirm that you feel that way.

Helping Your Child Control Anger and Other Emotions

Sometimes, some children become aggressive in an unknown reason. They hit, bite, push, and shove, which leads to hurting other people. You don't want your child to keep up this behavior, so knowing how to stop it today should be a good help.

Parenting is never easy and parents are all humans. Each time your child expresses himself in a rebellious way, you are feeling much stress. Talking about this matter should be a great help for parents facing openly insolent children or when coping with aggressive kids.

This is not an easy thing to deal with and it is simply easier said than done in several cases. However, the little methods disclosed in this chapter should help you stay calm and cool whenever you child pushes those alert button. These methods are as follows:

- Count to Ten. This might sound funny yet it really works wonders. Allow your child to see this as you do it. As you do the counting, take deep slow breaths. In addition, image yourself as calm, while going through the scenario with good results.

- Show Some Authority. Determine that nobody has the true authority over you except when you allow them. Furthermore, it is your choice to get upset or angry. Keep yourself reminded that if you give away more power, your insolent child will have less power to take from you. There is nobody else, but you will hold the key to your individual actions.

- Always Monitor Your Progress. Create a list of the incidents wherein you have been successful when coping with aggressive behavior of children. And then, if you seem to falter, just keep yourself reminded of the good times when you've prevailed in and get the best of the situation.

- Tell Yourself that It Won't Last Long. Always remind yourself that it won't last more than a couple of moments. Think that it will simply pass and that nothing would last forever. And, your child will eventually grow up, whether defiant or aggressive, more likely quicker than you actually like them to.

- Feel Good For Being Responsible. Keep yourself reminded of how good it feels to take responsibility for your emotional reactions. Give yourself some time for positive thoughts and feelings.

- Always Take Things Positively. Consider the idea that someone else always takes it more difficult than you and that your experience can't be compared to what somebody else may have. Remember that a greater trial, the more fulfilling and greater the triumph would feel. Make use of it as your motivation until you get there, and eventually, you will.

- Don't Respond To Aggression With Aggression. Keep in mind that responding to aggressive behavior with another aggressive behavior is never a good idea. This will just validate and enforce the behavior of the child. Your child desperately wants to become just like you and he or she would imitate any attitude you show.

- Become An Example. If you want to teach your child with good behaviors, you will need to practice the things you preach so as to guide his misbehavior effectively in the correct direction. Always teach and show your capability to manage your emotions. Keep in mind that the spotlight strikes on you. Hence, each time you feel enticed to curse or yell, stop and then reconsider that line of thinking.

- Teach Your Child The Alternatives. Show and teach your child some alternative techniques to manage his emotions. Provide approaches that are more constructive and more positive. Let him learn the ways to direct his emotions with creative expression. Encourage him to inform you whenever he feels upset or angry when possible.

- Recognize Their Efforts Consistently. Providing kids some reason to like changing is normally as simple as sharing affirmative recognition. No matter what, always remember that every child demands attention. Bad attention is quite better than totally no attention. Always provide your support, and apply positive encouragement with your efforts whenever possible. All those methods mixed with positive encouragement should aid you in shaping an aggressive child into the more controlled and developed person.

These tips mentioned above are only a few of the many ways that you can use to stay with composure when coping with aggressive kids. You have all the capability to stay calm when coping with aggressive kids and what it only takes is to know the best ways to respond in advance. When it comes to parenting, you will certainly appreciate the outcome of using the most applicable information available for dealing with misbehaving children. It doesn't need to be very hard, as all you really require is some fresh perspectives.

Furthering Child Anger Management

Just about every child feels angry seldom, yet when angry, negative comments and aggressive acts become a norm. It is crucial for parents to do the right action to aid their children. Parents may help their children learn to deal with their emotions and display anger in proper ways. Learn how to make it happen in this chapter.

A lot of child behavior issues focus on kids struggling with anger management. Disrespect, conflict, aggression and oppositional behavior may normally be alleviated through helping your kids know better handling of their anger. Once you teach your child with effective anger management skill, this will develop behavior, while providing him one of the most essential skills in life.

If you want your child to become a better person, teaching him how to better manage his anger is important. Start today by considering the following pointers:

Distinguish between Behavior and feelings

Normally, children face difficulty in knowing and understanding the distinction between aggressive behavior and feelings. Let your child know about feelings, allowing them to learn verbalizing the feelings of disappointment, frustration and anger. Basically, feelings, such as hurt and sadness are covered by aggressive behaviors. Teach the child how to determine and verbalize his feelings rather than acting them out.

Furthermore, mention that feeling angry is fine. Anger is similar to some other emotion. Just know the right times when to feel it.

Considering this will help children understand that discussing anger and feeling angry are not bad.

Mold Proper Anger Management Skills

It is important for you to become a role model of appropriate behaviors, teaching them the better management of their anger. When your child sees you losing your control, he will be more likely to experience trouble dealing with his own anger or distinguishing what's right from wrong.

There are times when parents choose to hide their frustrations and feelings from their children. Even though it is right to protect children from adult issues, they also have to witness just how you manage your feeling of anger. Produce chances to discuss feelings and allocate right ways to cope with them. Citing some instances when you get frustrated can teach children how to discuss their feelings.

Be responsible for your own behavior, especially when you lose control in front of your kids. Say sorry and talk about what should be done instead.

Implement Anger Rules

When it comes to anger, most families preset informal family rules regarding the acceptable and unacceptable behaviors. Other families do not mind slammed doors or raised voices, while some might have less acceptance for those behaviors. Make written home rules, which clarify kids the things they could do when they are angry and the kinds of behavior that might lead to certain consequences.

Anger rules must focus on respectfully behaving towards others. Children have to realize that only because they are angry does not give them the authority to hurt anybody. Deal with areas, like name calling, physical aggression and property destruction, so they know that they cannot throw and break things, or punt physically or verbally when they are mad.

Educate Healthy Approaches to Manage Anger

Children have to be aware of the right way to cope with anger. Rather than simply telling, "Don't hurt your sister", say what they should do when feeling frustrated. Use time out as discipline rather than punishment. This way, kids will learn taking breaks by themselves, helping them to cool down.

Children may also take advantage from knowing some coping skills. Let them learn how to take breaks when they are frustrated. Demonstrate to them some relaxation techniques through doing some enjoyable activities. Furthermore, you may teach them some problem-solving skills, while helping them know how to resolve conflicts calmly. Most especially, tell them to walk out when they are angry to avoid being aggressive.

Give Consequences When Needed

Children demand positive consequences once they follow anger rules, while they need negative consequences once they break them. Positive consequences are particularly crucial for children, who normally face hardships with anger management. A token economy or reward system may offer additional incentive to aid them to stay calm and apply their skills for managing their anger safely.

For any aggressive behavior presented, there has to be direct consequences. Based on the age of your child, consequences might include loss of privilege, time out or even restitution payment through performing additional chores or giving a toy to his victim.

It is just normal for children to have a hard time when managing their anger sometimes. However, this difficulty in anger management might result to some serious issues for some children in the long run. When the concern about the behaviors of your child or child anger management issues grows, seeking professional assistance is recommended. A knowledgeable and skilled professional may rule out any fundamental psychological health concerns and may provide producing a behavior or anger management plan.

Chapter 4- The Other External Factors Affecting Your Emotional State

When you are emotional, there are other things that you have to consider, and these will include your surroundings and circumstances. By taking these things into account, it will be much easier for you to balance your emotions not only based on what you feel but also based on those around you.

When you are surrounded by noise, clutter and chaos, it is only natural for you to feel irritable and stressed all day. In the end, it is definitely hard to find some moments for self-reflection and self-awareness when your surroundings and the circumstances around you is not conducive to Zen and relaxation. In the same way, it can be hard to cope with your problems when all that you see around are people that rush here and there, vehicles that speed away at a neck breaking speed, and a dizzy whirl of commerce that goes nonstop. You will surely wish that you have the power to slow things down just so you can feel much lighter.

When taking note of your surroundings and circumstances, it is a must for you to understand how your environment can affect your emotions. Your are surrounded by tons of stressors and if you will not take extra care, you might unnecessarily end up exposing yourself to the risk factors that can lead to mental health problems, something that you will surely not want to happen in your case. It is also advisable that you include management of your surroundings as a part of your agenda when taking care of your emotional wellbeing.

So, how will you create a good environment that can help improve your emotions?

There is a scientific explanation to the effect of color on the mood or emotion of a person. Various colors emit various light frequencies and these can all affect the emotions of people in different ways. If you like to de-stress, it is best to expose yourself to plenty of blue as this is known for helping in decreasing the blood pressure of a person. Meanwhile, yellows can inspire happiness so ensure that your surrounding has spatters of yellow. But, stay away from reds for these are known for triggering aggression and anger and even hypertension.

Color Your Space Green to Remind You of Nature

Humans need contact with nature. It has been found out that seeing life around you can give you a relaxing feeling and it also provides chemicals required for zeroing out stress that you can get through exposure to trees, plants and animals. Make sure that you take a regular stroll in the park or put some potted plants by your desk or window. Mother Nature offers free and accessible ways for making your emotions better and it is a must to make the most out of them.

Privacy is a Great Deal

A certain study discovered that an open lay out in offices are not conducive to the productivity and focus of workers. Cubicles are needed for privacy for you not to get distracted by what other people in front of, behind, or beside you are doing. The insecure feeling that comes from the feeling that someone is constantly watching you can be the cause of stress. If you are working, ask for some privacy not to be uppity but to take care of your emotional health.

Rapid Weather Changes Affect the Emotions

Climate change is becoming more evident than ever and based on research, the rapid changes in weather conditions can have an effect on your emotions. For example, heat waves have become longer, stronger and more often than what they used to and the onset of these can have an impact people who are already emotional. Anxiety and stress can also happen when there is an impending disastrous weather condition, particularly for those that leave near the vulnerable areas. Knowing how changes in the climate can result to emotional problems is the initial step to prevent the start or worsening of emotional concerns.

Chapter 5- Mastering Pleasant Responses for all Situations

There are instances when you do not know how to react or respond to a certain situation. Should you be angry? Should you resent? Should you be happy or satisfied? When facing a difficult situation, it is important that you brainstorm the different responses that are available for you in order to handle things properly.

Conflicts will always be a part of your life. At times, these conflicts take place just when you least expect them. But remember that all conflicts can always be resolved when handled and dealt with properly.

Keeping Emotions in Check

The process of conflict resolution should actually start with controlling your emotional response. Some people might say that they react that way because they can't help it; but the truth is self-control is more than possible.

During difficult situations, you and you alone have the power to choose your responses. There might be occasions when you will lose control. This is pretty much understandable but at the end of the day, you need to simply accept responsibility for your response before you work to keep yourself under complete emotional control from that specific point forward. You have to set the example that others can follow. Since the emotional system of humans takes majority of its input from the external sources, you might as well influence other people to control their emotional state at the same time. When brainstorming your responses, you must not only deal with your own response but also set the tone for others to follow as this can lead to a better environment around you.

Evaluate Before You React

As it so happens, your emotions are things that you create on your own but can be affected by other external factors. When you simply find it hard to rein in your feelings, it is best that you assess first the available options that are available before you react to a certain situation.

When things are not going your way, it is just too easy for you to be angry or irritated. If you have a lot of work to do and your internet connection is giving you a hard time, you will surely fire up and before you know it, your emotions have already taken over your system.

With the demands of today's fast paced life, it is just too common to see other people reacting impulsively to situations without really bothering to stop and evaluate things first. And when things are done on impulse, you can only expect that results will not be good and can even make the situation even worse.

For instance, when the internet connection in your office is not working just when you have tons of deadlines to finish on your desk, what should you do? Should you flare up and start throwing things? Will you shout and be the cause of commotion in the office? Will you just walk out of the office just like that?

Even though this kind of reactions are understandable especially when you have reached the critical level of your emotions, this do not really lessen your problem and instead, it will only further aggravate the issue which can soon backfire on no one else but you.

Instead of reacting, the best thing that you can do is sit down and start to evaluate the options that are available. You can call the internet provider directly or you can talk to your superior to see if you can at least do something about your deadlines and still be able to finish all your work for the day.

You see, things are really not as complicated as they are if you will be more rational and reduce being emotional. At the end of the day, there are plenty of options available and the only thing that you need to do is to stop, relax and clear your mind of your negative emotions. This way, the issue will be solved and you can get back on track without causing any serious damage to yourself and to those around you.

Balanced Emotions Need Clear Decisions

If you want your emotions to be balanced, one of the things that you need to do is to decide on the perfect route that you need to take.

Many people tend to assume that emotions only happen to you and just like storms, the best that you can do is to just wait until these completely pass.

However, unlike those climatic storms, you can actually influence or even alter your emotions with no need to resort to different unhealthy methods such as drugs or alcohol. Having the ability to influence or manage your emotions can be a powerful marker to achieve good health, an emotional maturity as well as overall happiness.

Instead of letting yourself be swallowed up in your emotions, the perfect thing that you can do is decide on the right route that you need to take. It means that you need to find some diversions. For instance, when you feel bored or flat, just sitting in front of the TV with its uninteresting show will only worsen things. Instead, switch this off and go for a walk around your neighborhood. A breath of fresh air can help a lot in inevitably changing your mood.

If you feel angry, you can focus on the three essential things in your life that you feel grateful. In case you are anxious, you can imagine that the thing that makes you anxious has already took place and has gone much better than what you expect.

Controlling your emotions is possible and it is even made easier when you are able to pinpoint the right route that you should take. All you need is to think or do something entirely different. Never be passively carried along by your present emotion and instead, let your mind work properly to steer you towards the right path.

CHAPTER 6- LONG-TERM EASY-TO-DO-TRAINING ON COMMANDING AND MASTERING EMOTIONS

At what time you go to the gym you begin to train the muscles, joints, and overall body. During the process you start working out three times each week, starting the first session at 15 minutes, working up to one half hour, and gradually working out one hour three times per week. You have your equipment picked out, which includes all equipment that works on each section of your body. Gradually, you start feeling good, looking, good, and ready to reach the top of the world.

Likewise, the mind requires training in order to gain control, feel good and ready self to reach the top of the world. What you feed the mind comes out in your behaviors. If you feed the mind bad, thus bad will reveal itself, now, later, or sometime down the road.

Gradually, the emotions and mind will obey mischief and bad, until one day you find yourself in a miserable life wondering what happen along the way. Likewise, if you conform to acting out on the bad that you feed your mind, you will gradually run into trouble.

We can look at a few examples of someone with a guilty conscious. This person thought bad, acted bad, and now feeling bad as a result. Furthermore, he does not have control of his mind; rather his mind controls his every move, word, action, etc.

Consider:

Two couple marries, and somewhere down the road, the mate starts up an extra marital affair. He hides it for some time believing in his mind that he won't be caught. The truth comes out in our lives somewhere down the road. All the lies a person tells will catch up with him or her later. The light will shine and others will see those lies. This man is caught dead in his track. His wife instead of yelling, screaming, and making the situation grow worse, says nothing. She shoots him painful glares as he makes eye contact with her. She continues her days and nights acting as a wife, yet she refuses to engage sexually with her husband. Now, he is unaware at the moment that the wife knows about his affair.

A few weeks pass, and the wife shows her husband a trail of his unrighteous actions. She confronts him finally. As she does, he tries to deny what he has done, and she says to him. "I am not dim-witted, don't you act dim-witted either." He breaks down. He starts accusing his wife, making excuses and blaming her for his affair. He is dead wrong and knows it, yet it feels better at the minute for him to cast the blame. Finally, he tells her that he will put an end to the relationship, because he doesn't want to lose his wife. He swears to try hard to undo all the pain, hurt, sorrow, miserably, grief, and acts that did not include love.

What do see? You see a cheating man with low morals, values, standards, and maturity. This person harmed his family by acting out on his selfish desires. Now, emotions are packed in this scene, yet what do you see?

The wife is commanding and mastering her emotions. It shows in her actions, since instead of blowing up, she slowly addressed the problem. As she addressed the problem, she acted maturely. This woman has a trained conscious mind. The man on the other hand, has many problems within, and requires daily mind training in order to become the master of his mind, so that he can command his emotions. Train those emotions!

Putting a Stop to the Emotional Circus

Train that mind. If you want to command and master your emotions, you will need to train the mind accordingly. We wander through life learning along the way. As we learn, we toss the information in our mind like salads to shred through the details, locating the facts. What seems real to your mind? What is logical? What is reasonable? What are the facts? These are a few questions you may want to ask self. The questions can help, you learn to command and train the emotions, to master the mind. .

Life is either hard or bearable. We all make our own life, i.e. we try, and others will pose on our lives attempting to tear us down. We have to battle each day to conquer the enemies in our way, i.e. the people that are friends, which show enemy traits. People sometimes get in our way unknowingly and for no particular purpose.

To train the mind, you must understand that self-control, hope, confidence, self-esteem, self-assurance, and all those other words fit into the equation. The more you build on your human requirements, the higher the possibility you will grow toward mastering and commanding your emotions.

Let's consider how these humane qualities fit into the equation of mastering and commanding the emotions. What does it take to build self-esteem? Self-esteem firstly, is confidence and a satisfying feeling of being self. As you can see as you work to build your confidence, you will build self-esteem in the meantime. Confidence is a little bit more difficult, since you have to become aware of your inner powers. This is not always easy. However, you can monitor self closely at each task you handle while previewing and reviewing the details to see what you come up with, and each time you achieve move ahead after rewarding self.

Rewards don't mean to go out and buy a new car each time you do a good deed. Rather, just smiling, doing the fist/elbow move and saying "Yes," aloud could be your reward. It is showing you recognize self-actions and deeds and it is bringing power to the mind. Confidence is also learning to rely on self. Thus, it brings us to independence, which is a human requirement. This feature of our characteristics works hand in hand with all other requirements of humans.

Confidence is also a faith. This faith is a self-assurance that a person believes in self and his or her abilities to achieve. Confidence also includes certainty of one's words, actions, abilities, etc. If you have certainty then likely you have built on finding facts that promote convictions. Convictions are power beyond the norm power, since it, shows you are fact packing based. Confidence also builds trust, i.e. people will trust you as well as you trusting self.

Confidence is a cool mind that feels the freedom to make the next move without feeling doubt. Doubt is one of the major elements that cause people to feel emotional strung out. If you have doubts, guilt, hate, anger and the like instilled in your mind, thus the mind is the master and commander of you. You want to learn positive things to build during the process of becoming the master of your mind, while commanding your emotions. Sometimes the mind will play tricks, making you think you have confidence when you do not. This is a superficial display, thus check the training, and mind often to train the emotions. This will help you stay in charge of your mind and emotions, rather than falling back into the same patterns.

The Needed Building Blocks to Emotional Stability

The building blocks are elements we choose to incorporate in our life. Rather the building blocks are already there, yet it takes you to build those elements. Building blocks include pieces of our lives that have been shredded through life's tumbles and falls. For instance, if you recently come out of a bad relationship, you will need to reconstruct the pieces to make you a whole person again. This helps you to learn control, which helps to command and master the emotions. Most people in my area are unwilling to give love a second, third, fourth, fifth, sixth and the list goes on, giving it another chance. They often say, "I've been there; done that; don't want to do it again." Alternatively, they say, "I tried love; it didn't work, so now I am out to have fun." Their emotions rule them.

As you stumble and fall throughout your lifetime, you are tearing down the human qualities, mechanisms and the like the pastes you together. Some of those qualities include confidence, self-esteem, self-assurance, hope, faith, and the like. Once these qualities and elements of human makeup are torn apart, it often takes great effort to build the blocks. The problem is doubts set in, inferiority complexes arise, guilt takes over, grief, and blaming steps in the door, thus tearing you down. Thus, the emotions become the rulers.

Since we have considered a breakdown in relationships, let's consider inferiority. Inferiority is a critical significant view of personal inadequacy, which often is a consequence either in diffidence or from overcompensating in overstatement. In other words, the person will compensate by placing higher value of self in one area, while recognizing flaws in another area. This person has a self-esteem problem. Often counselors will deem inferiority complex issues as an exaggeration. This is not always true, since background has something to do with it. Someone in this person's life has degraded, put down, torn down, and shredded this persons humane mechanisms, thus the exaggeration in most instances is placed on counselors. However, the person has a degree of exaggeration, since many of these people have abilities, qualities and the like the surpass others.

Overall, inferiority complexes are collections of national inferiorities, cultural and provincial accumulations. How to you build on inferiority to control the mind and command the emotions? First, you look in the mirror and start changing the things about you that you want changed about others. This will help you build confidence and self-esteem, which can wipe out those inferiorities. The problem is media, television, and the world as a whole places high emphasis on sexy, sexuality and the like, thus it has created nothing more than an ongoing chain of problems; and inferiority complex is on that list.

Now, let's say you had recently left a bad relationship. What do you need to rebuild or reconstruct to make you complete again? Do you feel guilty? Do you believe it is your fault the breakdown occurred? If so then you must realize it takes two to tangle.

Keeping Emotions in Check

Consider what the mate has done throughout the relationship without blaming. Do you feel grief? Do you feel less than adequate? Do you feel attractive? Are you blaming him or her for the failure? Are you taking any responsibility for the let down? Do you have doubts of your abilities? Do you feel like you will never give love another try?

You must move these blocks from your path to build the mind, learn to master, and command the emotions.

CHAPTER 7- YOU CAN BE NATURALLY HAPPY

The last but definitely not the least thing that you have to do in order to achieve optimum emotional balance is to learn how to be happy with yourself. Of course, your emotions will never be put in their right places when you yourself are not happy and satisfied in your own skin. In this last chapter, you will learn some easy ways on how to embrace happiness within yourself.

Did you ever find yourself standing in front of the mirror feeling hateful and resentful of yourself? Do you really understand how it is to be totally disgusted with yourself, feeling the longing for changes?

There are times when you feel upset about something and you allow the circumstances and environment to dictate whether you will be happy or not. But the stark truth is that if you live your life with happiness and choose what you will do all that it takes so that you can be happy, it is very possible for you to be happy when you put your mind to it.

Happiness is something that you have to do on purpose. Even in the middle of difficulties and struggles, you have to choose to be happy. It is not something that comes from having things or other material things because happiness stems from within you. Being happy with yourself simply means that you have to show mercy to yourself, forgive yourself, befriend yourself, accept yourself, and last but not the least, love yourself.

It is a lifetime journey that calls for regular self-examination as well as a continuous process of making peace with yourself. It is all about discovering the things that make you unhappy and opting to live in true peace. This means that you treat yourself with kindness and compassion. This makes you start to enjoy your life even more, celebrating this to be a peaceful adventure. This helps you to live your life to the fullest, allowing you to make the whole world a much better place not only for you but also for others.

However, learning to be happy with who you are might be among the trickiest challenges that are going to face. For some people, such challenges can be too hard to handle, which is why they just let these rule their lives. There are also those who endure challenges but some choose to overcome them yet they do not have any idea how to do it.

If you want to be happy with yourself, here are some things that can help you out:

Self-Forgiveness

You have to forgive yourself for having negative thoughts. Forgive yourself for not thinking twice and for talking. Forgive yourself for showing rudeness to your superior, parents, friends and siblings. Never think of negative thoughts about yourself for the wrong decisions or wrong steps. It is a type of thinking that will put your focus on the issue and not on the solution. It will be best that you say good things regarding yourself instead of saying negative things. Say positive things to yourself for it will be a sign that you already forgave yourself.

Don't Talk and Think about Your Issues

Try to focus instead on the good in all situations that you face and all persons that you have relationships with, which include yourself.

Forgive Other People

If you like to make peace with other people, forgive, forget and learn to let go of the things that happened in the past. Holding grudges and resenting is never good. To forgive easily, assume that they did no cause offense to you in the first place.

Be Busy

When you are busy, you will have less time to think particularly of someone or something that cause your negative feelings. Getting your hands full will keep the negative thoughts from triggering you over and over again

Be a Blessing to Other People

Get your thoughts off yourself and instead, focus on being a blessing to those around you. Being a blessing to others results to more blessings coming back to you. This is an amazing phenomenon that not all people understand. Remember that life is not about receiving but more of giving.

Develop a Hobby

You can choose to spend your free time on listening to movies, reading, watching movies and other kinds of activities. These will help take your mind off the issues in your life and thoughts that you have concerning yourself.

Accept Who You Are

Never focus on things about yourself which you cannot control. Never strive to become someone else. Never care about what other people say or think about you when you are not even sure if they are wrong or right. Once you do this, you will be able to free yourself of anxiety and stress. Accept who you are, be contented and hope to become a much better you.

Don't Lose Hope

Remember that even the darkest tunnels have a light at the end. Hope is the one thing that you can never afford to lose and with this, you can take the path towards your happiness. This reminds you that things will be alright. With hope, you will be secured that whatever looks terrible is just a temporary occurrence and soon enough, things are going to turn out fine.

Be happy with yourself and soon enough, your emotions will be balanced out perfectly and success will be within easy reach.

About the Author

Kimberly holds a degree in Psychology and has been in practice for 10 years. She has helped many people control their emotions. She is an expert in child psychology as well as in marriage and relationship counselling.

Kim travels the world with her partner, Mia.